Xtreme Athletes
Shaun White

Xtreme Athletes

Shaun White

Jeff C. Young

MORGAN REYNOLDS

PUBLISHING

Greensboro, North Carolina

Xtreme Athletes

Michael Phelps
David Beckham
Danica Patrick
Kelly Slater
Shaun White

XTREME ATHLETES: SHAUN WHITE

Copyright © 2009 by Jeff C. Young

Library of Congress Cataloging-in-Publication Data

Young, Jeff C., 1948-
  Xtreme athletes : Shaun White / by Jeff C. Young.
    p. cm.
  Includes bibliographical references and index.
  ISBN-13: 978-1-59935-081-3
  ISBN-10: 1-59935-081-5
  1. White, Shaun, 1986- 2. Snowboarders--United States--Biography. I.
Title. II. Title: Shaun White.
  GV857.S57Y68 2008
  796.939092--dc22
  [B]

                                           2007047791

Printed in the United States of America

First Edition

To my sister Laurinda Hundley because she deserves a book of her own

Contents

Shaun White
(Courtesy of AP Images)

one

First Descent

In 2006, the attention of sports fans worldwide was focused not on a quarterback or soccer star, but on a gangly American teenager named Shaun White. Though he was barely out of high school, and had previously only been known to a small pocket of extreme sports fans, Shaun grabbed the world's attention as the star competitor on the U.S. Olympic Snowboarding Team. He was described in a newspaper profile:

> Shaun White is everything one would expect in an X Games athlete competing in this weekend's anti-establishment sports festival in Aspen, Colorado. The world's best snowboarder is a millionaire at nineteen,

a recent high school graduate who received academic credits for refinancing his $600,000 home and designing the graphics on his signature line of Burton snowboards. He has won three cars this year but is too young to rent one. His nickname is "The Flying Tomato," a reference to the unruly mop of red hair that sticks out of his Led Zeppelin-blaring, iPod- equipped helmet.

Though Shaun was about to become one of the world's greatest athletes, he barely lived past his first birthday. When he was born in San Diego, California, on September 3, 1986, Shaun Roger White was diagnosed with a heart condition known as tetralogy

Diagram of a normal and a deformed heart

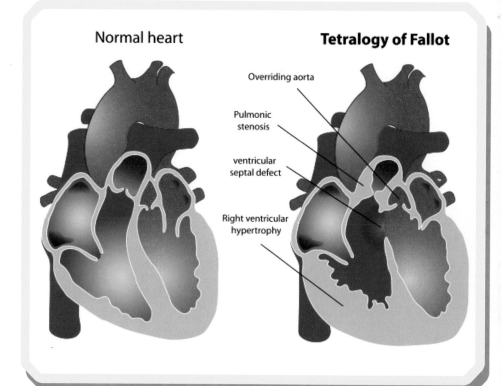

of Fallot, a relatively common heart defect which negatively affects the amount of oxygen in a person's blood. Before his first birthday, Shaun underwent open heart surgery twice; the surgeries were a success and corrected the condition.

Shaun was the last of three children born to Roger and Cathy White. Shaun's brother, Jesse, is seven years older and his sister Kari is one year older.

Shaun stands with his family (from left to right): mother Cathy, sister Kari, Shaun, brother Jessie, and father Roger. (*Courtesy of Mike Powell/Getty Images*)

Shaun's father was an avid surfer, and his grandparents on his mother's side were both pro-skaters in the roller derby. Clearly, Shaun inherited much of his family's athleticism, and his parents never discouraged him from taking up extreme sports.

[My mother] tells these stories of when I was a baby and how she could only hold my foot because of these operations and stuff, and I think that takes a lot for a parent to almost lose their kid and then let them go out on a snowboard or skateboard. I mean I don't land [perfectly] all the time. When I was learning how to snowboard, I got knocked out, broke my hand, my foot; I fractured my skull with one crash. It's been a trip for [my parents] as well.

As a young child, Shaun loved jumping up and down on his parents' trampoline, thrilled to be in the air. Then, when he was six years old, Shaun began skateboarding.

"I rode on my knees when I first started at age six," Shaun recalled. "Then one day, my older brother said, 'Let's race.' It was like, 'You can't beat me.' He kicked super hard and beat me. So I thought, I've got to stand up."

When Jesse would go to the nearby skate ramp, Shaun would tag along. Jesse and his friends would tell the pesky little brother that he wasn't good enough to do the same tricks that they did. Shaun grew determined to prove them wrong.

"[Jesse] would say, 'Oh, you can't do tricks like those guys.' That gave me a push to succeed. . . . By the end of the first day, I was doing fakie rocks and little pop airs."

A few months before taking up skateboarding, Shaun had already begun to snowboard. The White family took frequent ski trips, and Shaun was instantly attracted to the thrill of strapping on skis and rushing down the mountainside. His mother remembers that Shaun was "crazy on skis," and when he became interested in snowboarding, she hoped that Shaun would slow down a bit when he got on a snowboard. "Maybe on a snowboard he'll sit on his butt and go slow," Cathy said.

However, when Shaun wanted to learn how to snowboard, he was held back because of his age. The Whites often traveled to Bear Mountain, a popular ski resort in California. That's where Shaun became fascinated with snowboarding.

He wanted to take lessons, but the resort wouldn't give them to anyone younger than twelve. The Whites

The slopes of Bear Mountain Resort in California, where Shaun first learned to snowboard *(Courtesy of Big Bear Mountain Resorts)*

got around that by having Roger take the lessons. Then, after each lesson, he would teach Shaun what he had learned.

Shaun was a natural on the board, almost instantly possessed of the balance and skill needed to be a successful boarder. By the end of his first day of snowboarding, Shaun was attempting jumps. Jesse noticed that his younger brother might be some kind of a prodigy.

"Mozart was supposed to play piano," Jesse said. "It was that kind of a deal."

The Whites made snowboarding excursions a family activity. They would climb into the family van and travel to snowboarding competitions, where Kari also competed. She was the U.S. Open Junior Halfpipe champion in 2000.

Along with being a naturally talented athlete, Shaun was always a fierce competitor. The first time he played in a youth soccer game, he assaulted an opposing player with a flying kick to his chest. His competitiveness even carried over to playing board games.

"I gotta win all the games," Shaun said. "Everybody makes fun of me because I really get into it. We had Monopoly matches from hell where you don't really talk to each other afterwards."

With his family's support, Shaun was able to enroll in a snowboarding camp in Oregon. Tim Windell, the camp's director, thought about rejecting Shaun's application because Shaun was so young. But when he saw how good Shaun was, he quickly changed his mind.

"We almost didn't take him, because he was only six or seven at that time," Windell recalled, "and we'd never had such a young camper. But he was an incredible athlete, even at that point in time."

By the time that he was seven, Shaun felt that he was ready to start competing. His mother convinced Burton Snowboards to sponsor her young son, and Shaun entered and won his first amateur snowboarding contest. The victory qualified him to compete in the twelve-and-under division of the United States Amateur Snowboard Association's (USASA) National championships. Shaun finished in eleventh place, which would be one of his lowest finishes in any snowboarding event—amateur or pro.

Soon, Shaun was winning every amateur competition he entered; he won every amateur competition around for "like five years in a row," he recalled. Before turning pro, Shaun won five national snowboarding titles in the twelve-and-under division.

While traveling and competing in snowboarding competitions, Shaun still managed to enjoy a relatively normal life. "Whenever I'm at school or anything, or with my friends, snowboarding's like the last thing we ever talked about," Shaun said. "You know, it would be like 'oh, dude, that teacher's so mean,' you know, normal stuff."

Shaun believed that the best way to improve was by competing against pros instead of amateurs. Since he had routinely dominated the amateur competition,

Shaun competing in a 2001 Snowboard World Cup event (*Courtesy of Al Bello/Allsport*)

there was nothing else left for him there; he turned pro at age thirteen.

Along with the promise of tougher competition, turning pro meant that Shaun could start winning prize money and signing endorsement deals. Shaun's family had always been supportive, but the cost of travel and equipment was a major drain on their finances. Shaun's father was a city employee and his mother worked as a waitress. Neither parent made much money, and they were spending up to $20,000 a year to subsidize Shaun and Kari's snowboarding.

"My family took out a $50,000 loan on their house just to help me get started," Shaun said. "And that was when snowboarding wasn't anything—the X Games had just started."

When they traveled to take Shaun and Kari to snowboarding events, they would save money by sleeping in their van.

> We would shower at rest stops, using milk cartons for the hot water. We prided ourselves on being more ghetto. We had this huge white van, and I remember that my dad stuck a pizza box over the radiator—it kept the heat in, or something. We would get to this superfancy upper-class ski resort, and some lady came out and said, "You can't park that thing here."

However, once Shaun turned pro, it didn't take long for his family to get a good return on their investment. During his first year as a pro, Shaun made a little bit of prize money with some top finishes. But in February 2000, Shaun took third place at the Nippon Open in Japan, winning a significant cash prize.

"I had made my parents' salaries combined, with that contest," Shaun recalled, "and it was amazing to me at that time."

But that would be just the beginning of a sensational career. X-Game fame, Olympic gold, and lucrative endorsement deals would follow. And it would all happen before Shaun even graduated from high school.

ROLLER DERBY

Shaun White was not the first athlete in his family: his mother's parents were pro skaters in the sport of roller derby.

One television critic described roller derby, by writing: "The sport, which sometimes seemed more like a head-bashing, free-for-all than a test of athletic skill, combined elements of skating, football, rugby, and wrestling." When Shaun's grandparents played, a roller derby player had to speedily roller skate around a banked track while showing a fearless disregard for their well being. Some people might consider it a forerunner of today's extreme sports.

Roller derby's roots go back to 1932 when a man named Leo Seltzer coined the name and envisioned an event that would combine roller skating with long distance endurance racing. Three years later, the first Trans-Continental Roller Derby was held in Chicago. Twenty-five two-player teams competed to roller skate a total distance of 3,000 miles on an oval track.

The marathon event began August 13 and finally ended on September 22. The teams skated for eleven and a half hours a day, and distance was tabulated by the number of laps they completed. Only nine of the twenty-five teams were able to finish the grueling event.

In 1937, Seltzer modified his creation after the noted writer Damon Runyon suggested that more physical contact was needed. Seltzer created the International Roller Derby League (IRDL). The fan base and interest increased after skaters began bumping, jostling, and scuffling with each other. A competing outfit called Roller Games was founded the same year. Roller Games tried to outdo the IRDL by ratcheting up the violence. The exaggerated violence was similar to the theatrics of professional wrestling.

From 1949 to 1951, roller derby was regularly broadcast on the ABC television network. At one time it was the network's most popular show. In the late 1950s, the sport enjoyed a resurgence in popularity when Leo's son, Jerry Seltzer, began filming the games and selling them to television stations. Jerry was able to get around 120 stations to broadcast roller derby on a regular basis.

The game is played by two five-skater teams with three positions: a jammer, three blockers, and a pivot. A pack of eight skaters composed of the blockers and the pivots begin skating. The pivots are like a pace car at the start of a NASCAR race. They lead the pack and set the pace. They are also allowed to act as blockers.

The two jammers attempt to catch up to the pack and then work their way through the pack. The blockers try to propel their jammer forward while blocking the opposing team's jammer. Points are scored when a jammer

passes an opposing team's skater. Additional points are scored if the jammer is able to lap the pack. The jockeying for position leads to a lot of crowd-pleasing physical contact.

Dwindling attendance and increasing transportation costs caused the IRDL to fold in 1973. In 1984, a strange new form of the sport called Roller Jam made its debut. It used a figure-eight shaped track, a pit of live alligators, and well-choreographed games with in-line skaters.

Roller Jam only lasted for two years. Since then, other roller derby teams and leagues have been founded that remain true to the sport's original rules.

Skaters participate in a roller derby in 1950. *(Library of Congress)*

The History of Snowboarding

Snowboarding is a recently developed sport that can trace its origins to three older sports—skateboarding, surfing, and skiing. A world-class snowboarder can get air and do acrobatic stunts like a skateboarder, glide over the snow like a skier, and change the direction of his ride like a surfer. Yet, it remains a unique sport and skill.

It's been claimed that a crude form of snowboarding was first practiced by children in the early 1920s. The kids used old barrel staves as makeshift snowboards. They would ride them sideways down snowy hills.

The prototype for the snowboards used today was designed and built in the mid-1960s by a Michigan skier and engineer named Sherman Poppen. Poppen made a new toy for his daughter by nailing a pair of kids' skis together and adding a steering rope to the front of the skis. He called it Snurfer since it combined the elements of snow skiing and surfing.

An advertisement for the Brunswick Snurfer (Courtesy of the Brunswick Corporation)

SHERMAN POPPEN

On Christmas day in 1965, Sherman Poppen was watching his daughter Wendy sledding in their backyard. Wendy was unsuccessfully trying to ride her sled while standing up. That gave Poppen an idea.

He went to the corner drug store and bought a pair of thirty-six inch skis. Poppen added a couple of wooden cross pieces to hold the skis together and added a rope to the front of the skis. The rope gave the rider something to grasp and helped to stabilize the skis.

Poppen's wife thought the invention should be called a Snurfer—a name that combined the words snow and surf. When the other neighborhood kids saw Wendy riding her Snurfer, they began pestering Poppen.

"And then the kids kept saying Mr. Poppen, make me one, make me one," Poppen recalled. "The reason that I did all that then, by the way, was that back then the thing for hot skiers to do was to kick off one ski and ski down on one ski. And I was never able to do that so I thought that this was the next best thing, so I started messing around with it."

Poppen soon found that he couldn't make them fast enough. But he was able to sell the manufacturing rights to the Snurfer to Brunswick, a major American sporting goods company. In return for the rights, Poppen received a royalty payment from Brunswick for every Snurfer the company sold.

According to Poppen, Brunswick sold more than 300,000 Snurfers before they discontinued sales. Other estimates claim that the figure was more than 1 million. Poppen doesn't say exactly how much money he made off of the Snurfer, but it was thousands of dollars.

"I built a lovely home with the royalties," Poppen said. "I called it the house that the Snurfer built."

When the first competitions using the Snurfer got started, the sport was called Snurfing instead of snowboarding. But that changed when a Vermont snurfer named Jake Burton Carpenter came out with a modified version of Poppen's Snurfer. It was called a Snurfboard. That led to a legal dispute between Burton and Poppen.

"Burton was calling his board Snurfboards and mine was a Snurfer," Poppen said, "and I didn't like that because he was taking my name away and I hired an attorney to tell him that, hey, that name is trademarked. Well, I wish that I hadn't done it now, because that's when the sport became snowboarding."

Although he doesn't snowboard, Poppen continues to be an avid skier and he enjoys watching snowboarders zoom down the slopes around his home in Steamboat Springs, Colorado. The lack of recognition for helping to launch a new sport doesn't seem to bother him. His reward comes from seeing how much fun snowboarders are having.

"I just love to watch them (snow-boarders) go through the trees in the powder, though," Poppen said. "Steamboat has great trees. I love to stand next to them in line, and they're all talking, and if they only knew who was standing next to them—I get a little silent vicarious thrill out of that."

Brunswick, a large American sporting goods company, bought the rights to Poppen's Snurfer and began manufacturing and selling it. They advertised the Snurfer as combining the thrills of skiing with the skills of surfing. It's estimated that Brunswick sold between 300,000 to 1 million Snurfers at around fifteen dollars each.

While the Snurfer was being sold other skateboarders and skiers began looking for ways to modify and improve the design and performance of Poppen's invention. The Snurfer was fun to ride, but it was hard to control, so in the 1970s a Vermont Snurfer enthusiast named Jake Burton Carpenter added rubber straps to Poppen's invention. That made it easier for the rider to stand and control the direction of the board. Today, his company, Burton Snowboards, is a well-known major manufacturer of snowboards.

Tom Sims, a New Jersey skateboarder, was another pioneer in improving the design and performance of the snowboard. Sims wanted to skateboard during the winter months, but the icy streets and sidewalks prevented that. During his junior high wood-shop class, Sims worked on modifying the design of the skateboard so it could glide across the ice. In 1977, he founded Sims

Snowboards, which has become another one of the sport's leading manufacturers.

In the early days of snowboarding, the biggest problem wasn't the design or the performance, it was getting acceptance from skiers and the management of ski resorts. Since the Snurfer had a bad reputation for being an unpredictable, out-of-control device, most ski resorts banned its use. Insurance companies routinely refused to sell liability policies to resorts that allowed snowboarding. Snowboarding was also hampered by the public perception of snowboarders: seen as free-spirited rebels with little use or respect for rules and authority figures, most establishments had no desire to allow them onto their premises.

As late as 1985, less than 10 percent of the ski areas and resorts in the United States allowed snowboarding, but ski resorts became more accepting after design modifications and special equipment made snowboards easier to control. Jake Burton Carpenter helped snowboarding to gain wider acceptance by giving demonstration and instruction programs. The addition of a certification program taught novice and experienced snowboarders safety, proper techniques, and the etiquette of sharing the slopes.

By 1995, very few resorts still banned snowboarding. Many had built half-pipes, the U-shaped incline used to get the riders airborne. Because of its roots in skiing, surfing, and skateboarding, manufacturers in those sports began introducing snowboarding equipment and

A half-pipe

apparel. They also started sponsoring events and riders, and producing videos.

As the sport became more acceptable, it also became more appealing and popular. The growth of the sport led to the creation of organizations to standardize events, rules, scoring, and rider rankings.

The first official American snowboarding competition was held in Leadville, Colorado, in 1981. During the 1980s, several snowboarding federations were formed in Europe and North America. The first governing body for American competition was the United States of America Snowboard Association (USASA). It was founded in 1988 with a five hundred dollar donation from the publishers of Transworld Snowboarding Magazine. One year later, the International Snowboard Association (ISA) was created to regulate and oversee international competitions.

In 1991 the ISA became the International Snowboard Federation (ISF). The influence of the ISF was eventually overshadowed by the Federation Internationale du Ski (FIS). The FIS gradually replaced the ISF as the sport's governing body because it was better at organizing competitions, signing up sponsors, and attracting

TV coverage and contracts. In 2002, the ISF disbanded.

1995 is regarded as a landmark year in the short history of the sport. That's when the International Olympic Committee (IOC) decided to make snowboarding an official Olympic event. The first medals were awarded during the 1998 Winter Olympics in Nagano, Japan. Athletes competed in three separate events—the half-pipe, the snowboard cross, and the giant slalom.

Chris Klug snowboards during the 1998 Winter Olympics in Nagano, Japan. *(Courtesy of AP Images/Robert F. Bukaty)*

Unfortunately, the first Winter Olympic snowboarding competitions were marred by some negative publicity. Canadian snowboarder Ross Rebagliati had his gold medal taken away after he tested positive for marijuana. He later got the medal back because the IOC had no policy at that time banning marijuana use. It was not considered to be a performance-enhancing drug.

Although the snowboarding events in the 1998 Winter Olympics were the first, the 2002 Winter Olympics in Salt Lake City are remembered as the Olympics that made the world take notice of the fast-growing sport. Shortly before the start of the 2002 competition, a magazine article noted:

> Once the province of body-pierced punks, the sport is now one of America's fastest-growing winter pursuits. Snowboarders accounted for 28.3 percent of 57.3 million visits to the slopes last season—up 25.9 percent from the year before. . . . Not bad for a sport that began a mere thirty-seven years ago when a Michigan man joined two skis together to create a snow-surfer, or Snurfer for his kids. . . . The demanding "tricks" in the supersize U-shaped course, known as a "half-pipe," combine the elegance of figure skating and the muscular moves of gymnastics—executed five to fifteen feet in the air. The parallel giant slalom, a

new event with side-by-side races, requires as much agility and speed as its ski equivalent.

In the 2006 Winter Olympics in Italy, American snowboarders accounted for six of their country's twenty-nine medals. Shaun White won the gold in the men's half-pipe and Hannah Teter won the gold

Shaun stands beside Hannah Teter *(Courtesy of AP Images/Jeff Christensen)*

in the women's half-pipe; Seth Wescott won a gold medal in the men's snowboard cross. American snowboarders also won three silver medals.

Teter and her silver medalist teammate, Gretchen Bleiler, reinforced the perception of snowboarders being a free-spirited, rebel breed. Just before making their medal run, they sneaked away to a roped off section so they could practice on some fresh snow.

"The guards were saying, 'You can't go,' so we just jumped under the ropes, strapped in quick and went," Bleiler said. "That's what snowboarding is all about. It's not about sticking to a routine."

Although snowboarding is still a freewheeling, freestyle kind of sport, it has become a safer one. One factor has been Shaun White's influence in getting riders to wear helmets. Even though Shaun has been nicknamed "the flying tomato" for his flowing red hair, he wears a protective helmet when he snowboards.

"When I was younger, nobody was wearing them," Shaun recalled. "It was lame to wear a helmet. Now it seems like everybody's wearing them."

There are no laws requiring snowboarders to wear helmets, and resorts don't insist on it, though they are required in Olympic and most pro

Shaun White was one of the first snowboarders to wear a helmet. (Courtesy of Buzz Pictures/Alamy)

competitions. According to the National Ski Areas Association, more skiers and snowboarders are wearing helmets, but there hasn't been a decrease in head injuries. In fact some studies claim that helmeted skiers and snowboarders are inclined to take greater risks.

Still, many parents are grateful to Shaun for setting a good example. "I've had parents say, 'My kid is so stoked you wear a helmet, because now he doesn't feel lame to wear one,'" Shaun said.

Snowboarding has become the fastest-growing winter sport in the USA. In 2004, snowboarders represented- around 20 percent of the visitors to American ski resorts. It's been predicted that by 2015, the number of snowboarders will overtake the number of skiers.

There is speculation that snowboarding will overtake skiing as America's No. 1 snow sport.

two

The Flying Tomato

In 1993, a management team at the TV sports network ESPN decided to create an international competition in some of the newer action sports. Ron Semiao, then the head of programming for ESPN, was credited for coming up with the idea. He knew that even though kids played and watched traditional sports like baseball, basketball, football, and hockey, many had become attracted to and were playing other newer sports. These newer sports were being called extreme sports because they involved an element of risk-taking that was lacking in the more traditional sports.

Sports like skateboarding, motocross, and BMX were attracting and exciting kids throughout the USA

Some sports are considered extreme because of the element of danger involved in doing them.

and the rest of the world. Young sports fans were becoming transfixed by these daredevil athletes. As writer Shelly Youngblut noted, these recklessly bold athletes were "defying both gravity and society's standards of reasonable risk."

In April 1994, ESPN held a press conference to announce that a new competition called the Extreme Games would be held the following year. For the first time, extreme athletes would have a worldwide stage for showcasing their talents.

The first Extreme Games were held at three different sites in Rhode Island and Vermont in June 1995. At that time, Shaun White was eight years old and was already competing in amateur snowboarding events. In the initial Extreme Games, athletes competed in twenty-seven events in nine sports categories. The new events included bungee jumping, skysurfing, skateboarding, bicycle stunt riding, and street luge.

The Extreme Games' popularity exceeded ESPN's expectations. More than 198,000 spectators attended the games while a worldwide audience of millions tuned in to watch them on TV. Among TV advertisers, male viewers from ages twelve to thirty-four are one of the most coveted demographics. The Extreme Games proved to be a huge hit with that all-important group. It soon became apparent to ESPN that the games needed

Street luge, a sport where the participant rides down a street, road, or paved course laying on a luge, was part of the first Extreme Games in 1995.

to be expanded. Originally, ESPN had announced that the games would be held every two years. But because of their immense popularity and acceptance, the games became an annual event.

To attract a bigger international audience, the name of the event was changed to the X Games. It was

Shaun competing in the 2001 X Games *(Courtesy of Al Bello/Allsport)*

also decided that, like the Olympics, there would be both summer and winter games. The first Winter X Games, held in Big Bear Lake, California, featured snowboarding, ice climbing, and snow mountain bike racing. The Winter Games were an immediate success. They were televised in 198 countries and territories in twenty-one different languages; the worldwide audience rivaled the Winter Olympics.

Although he began his pro snowboarding career in 1999, Shaun didn't participate in the X Games until 2001. Since then, he's been a medalist every year. After the 2007 X Games, Shaun had won a total of twelve medals—ten in snowboarding and two in skateboarding. From 2003 to 2006, he dominated the slopestyle event, winning four consecutive gold medals, and also won gold in the superpipe event.

Slopestyle is a judged event. A single rider goes through a series of jumps and other obstacles while performing various tricks. The superpipe is a variation of the half-pipe; the major difference is that the walls are six feet higher (seventeen feet compared to eleven in the half-pipe) and the pipe is longer and wider. This difference in the dimensions enables the riders to go higher.

After dominating snowboarding at the 2002 Winter X Games, Shaun seemed like a shoo-in for the U.S. Olympic team for the 2002 Winter Olympics. Though snowboarding had made its Winter Olympics debut four years earlier in 1998, Shaun didn't pay it much attention. Since he was only eleven then, he had other interests. "I was more into Power Rangers at that time," Shaun said.

But by 2002, Shaun was in his fourth year of being a pro snowboarder. He hoped to make the U.S.

Shaun performing at the 2003 X Games where he took home gold in both the slopestyle and superpipe events *(Courtesy of Donald Miralle/ Getty Images)*

Olympic team, but he didn't think it would come easily. He knew that there would be a high level of competition.

> I think [riders] did it the first year (1998) just for the experience. Like, you know, 'We'll give it a try.' But, whoa, it worked out, so now I think a lot of riders are going to go for it. The level of competition may be higher this time. I think that my competition is basically going to be [U.S. Riders] Danny Kass, Todd Richards, and Ross Powers.

Shaun was right about the high level of competition; he failed to make the team, losing by just three-tenths of a point. Instead of being in the Winter Olympics, he watched it on TV. The riders who beat him all won medals in the half-pipe: Ross Powers won the gold, Danny Kass took the silver, and Jarret Thomas got the bronze.

Only fifteen years old, Shaun knew that there would be other chances for Olympic medals and glory. He got over the setback and refocused on his pro career. His performance at the 2003 Winter X Games showed that he was back on track. Shaun won the gold in both the slopestyle and superpipe for the second straight year. With the prize money from the X Games and other

Shaun snowboarding in 2002. Although he failed to make the Olympic team that year, Shaun continued to focus on his professional snowboarding career. *(Courtesy of Jed Jacobsohn/Getty Images)*

events that he had won, Shaun bought a new house for his parents.

Although he was competing full time, Shaun was able to keep up with his school work. A combination of home schooling and a flexible curriculum earned Shaun enough school credits to keep up with his classmates.

Shaun graduated from Carlsbad Seaside Academy in Carlsbad, California, a school made up of advanced pupils with special circumstances. Kathy Heritage, who was one of Shaun's teachers there, remembers Shaun as an "unassuming, goal-oriented" student. Shaun received mostly A's and B's.

The school accommodated Shaun by giving him credits for things that he did outside of the classroom. The graphic designs that Shaun created for his line of Burton snowboards and clothes earned him an art credit. His snowboarding DVD, *The White Album*, got him a credit in video production. Refinancing the first house that he bought was good for a credit in economics; interviews with the media earned him a credit in English.

Even though he graduated with people his age, Shaun's experiences made him feel more mature than most of his classmates. "I definitely feel older than most kids my age," Shaun said. "Being on the road

Shaun talks with his teacher during a geometry lesson at Carlsbad Seaside Academy. *(Courtesy of ZUMA Press)*

since I was fourteen gives me a different perspective. Everyone older was teaching me about life. Plus, seeing the world, learning that there is more to life than just high school makes you mature a lot faster."

While he was finishing up with his formal education, Shaun was having one of the most successful seasons in the brief history of pro snowboarding. During the

Shaun soars through the air at the 2005 X Games. *(Courtesy of Jamie Squire/ Getty Images)*

2005-2006 Season, Shaun won every event that he entered. Shaun had five Grand Prix wins and two gold medals at the Winter X Games. Then at the U.S. Open, he won the half-pipe and slopestyle events.

None of these victories, though, prepared Shaun for the challenge and international focus he was about to face. At age nineteen, in 2006, he qualified for the U.S. Olympic Snowboarding Team. He was about to travel to Torino, Italy, to compete for his country and a place in Olympic history.

three

Olympic Glory

Though Shaun entered the 2006 Winter Olympics as a seasoned competitor, his early performance in Torino did not go smoothly. Whether it was due to stress over the expectations, the increased scrutiny of an international audience, or simply bad luck, Shaun fell while making his landing during his first qualifying run. The unexpected fall dropped him down to seventh place. Only the top six snowboarders would advance on to the final round of the medal competition. If he made another mistake, even a minor one, he would be eliminated.

"I was so mad at myself," Shaun said. "I really don't like falling but when the pressure's on, I always seem to go bigger and land everything better."

Shaun quickly regained his composure. While waiting for his next turn, he took a few easy rides with his coach. That cleared his head. When his turn came, Shaun was rested, ready, and determined.

In his next run, Shaun focused on what snowboarders call getting big air—making big jumps and not trying any overly risky acrobatic tricks. With the heavy metal sounds of AC/DC's "Back in Black" blasting in the background, Shaun soared skyward, then back down towards the half-pipe, making a graceful landing.

The judges gave Shaun a score of 45.3 out of a possible 50 points; it was the highest score of the day. Shaun advanced on to the medal round.

Before the final round, Shaun came down with a nosebleed. It wasn't brought on by anxiety or pressure, but by inhaling the dry mountain air in the Italian Alps. Shaun waved off a TV camera crew trying to get some video footage of his bloody nose. Then he rode his snowboard into the half-pipe.

Shaun started off by doing a frontside air, which led to a McTwist—a 540-degree inverted spin. He continued to wow the judges by adding a Cab 1080 (three rotations after starting off by riding backwards) and a backside 900 (two-and-a-half rotations after the rider turns his back into a spin) to his performance.

Shaun catches big air during his second qualifying run for the men's half-pipe at the 2006 Winter Olympics.

His landings were clean and controlled. The judges were impressed enough to give Shaun a score of 46.8. No one had gotten a higher score that day—and no one would. Shaun's American teammate, Danny Kass, came closest with a 43.8. After Finland's Markku Koski took a tumble on his final run, Shaun clinched the gold medal, and Kass won the silver.

When Shaun proudly stood on the podium to receive his medal, he was unable to hold back the tears. "I wasn't crying, dude," Shaun told an interviewer. "I had some tears come out."

At the age of nineteen Shaun could lay claim to the titles of Olympic champion and world's greatest snowboarder. Shaun accepted the accolades with a mixture of disbelief and humor.

"It hits you the next day," Shaun said. "You're like, 'Wow, did that seriously just happen? . . . I got a gold medal; I guess that I'm an athlete now. I gotta start going to the gym."

But Shaun wasn't joking when he talked about what winning an Olympic gold medal really meant to him, his family, and his fellow Americans.

"When I saw my mom crying, I realized how huge this was," Shaun recalled. "But [I didn't] just win for

Shaun stands on the podium after winning gold for the men's half-pipe competition during the 2006 Winter Olympics. *(Courtesy of AP Images/Lionel Cironneau)*

myself and my family. It was for everyone. When I came home, I heard, 'Thanks for bringing the gold home for us' [from] random people on the street. That was the coolest thing."

The History of Skateboarding

Skateboarding is a sport that has its roots in both roller skating and surfing. The first skateboards were made when kids used old roller skates to build homemade scooters.

Scooters were a popular toy but expensive because of their bicycle-type wheels. As early as the 1900s, inventive kids found that a cheaper model could be made by taking the wheels off of a roller skate and fastening them to the bottom of a piece of wood. One wheel would be fastened to the front and one to the rear. Then a wooden crate would be nailed to the front to be used as the handlebars.

Scooters like this one, made from putting roller skate wheels on a board, were the forerunners of the modern skateboard. (*Courtesy of Ralph Morse/Time Life Pictures/Getty Images*)

After a while, the riders found that it was more fun to remove the crate and balance themselves on the board. Since there weren't any skate parks at that time, the riders would look for slopes and hills.

During the 1950s, surfers found that these homemade skateboards gave them something to ride during winter months when they couldn't surf. The balance and stance needed to stay on a skateboard was similar to what it took to ride a wave.

A surfer named Bill Richards and his son, Mark, are credited with coming up with the idea of using homemade skateboards to go "sidewalk surfing." Other surfers followed their lead, and sporting goods manufacturers like Hobie, Humco, and Makaha began making and marketing skateboards.

By the mid-1960s, an estimated 50 million skateboards had been sold in America. The sport had become so popular that the 1965 International Skateboard Championships were featured on ABC's *Wide World of Sports*. That same year, *Life* magazine ran a cover story on skateboarding and called the skateboard "the most exhilarating and dangerous joy-ride device this side of the hot rod."

Two boys skateboarding during the mid-1960s. *(Courtesy of Harold M. Lambert/Lambert/Getty Images)*

As skateboarding became more popular, manufacturers began using different materials and coming out with different models for different styles of skateboarding. For the downhill riders, they made boards that were wider, longer, and more stable. Slalom skaters favored the shorter boards. Skateboarders who used empty swimming pools needed a combination of the two.

The introduction of a skateboard with a kicktail enabled skateboarders to start performing elaborate tricks.

One of the most significant modifications in skateboard design was the introduction of the kicktail—the curved back end of the skateboard—in the late 1960s. Invented by Larry Stevenson, the kicktail acts as a lever that enables the rider to lift and turn the skateboard. Many of the tricks that skateboarders perform today couldn't be done without using the kicktail.

About the same time that the kicktail was introduced, skateboarding's popularity took a sudden fall. It was seen as a risky and unsafe sport; the American Medical Association even denounced skateboarding, calling it "a new medical menace." Skateboard companies went out of business and stores quit stocking skateboards. Many people assumed that the skateboarding fad had died out.

But people continued to skateboard, even though parts became harder to find and some skateboarders reverted to using homemade boards. In the early 1970s the sport made a comeback. The resurgence in popularity came when a surfer named Frank Nasworthy invented wheels made from urethane—a firm, sturdy plastic—for skateboards.

Skate park in Davis, California *(Courtesy of Davis Wiki)*

A street skater *(Courtesy of Ian Walton/Allsport)*

Nasworthy's invention, along with the later addition of encased precision bearings inside the wheels, gave riders greater control of the board while traveling at higher speeds. It also made for a smoother ride, which allowed the rider to stay on the board longer. With this increased control, daring skateboarders began jumping over obstacles and doing midair twists and jumps.

In 1976, the first skate park in the USA opened in Florida. Over the next three years, an estimated additional three hundred parks opened. Skateboarders were also building their own plywood ramps and using empty swimming pools and concrete embankments.

The early 1980s saw many parks closing because of the skyrocketing costs of liability insurance. Empty swimming pools and plywood half-pipe ramps remained popular. But in places where those weren't available, skateboarders took to the streets. A style known as street skating evolved, in which skateboarders rode over or on curbs, railings, steps, and benches.

The early 1980s also saw the emergence of Tony Hawk as pro skateboarding's first superstar. Hawk won his first pro competition in 1982 when he was fourteen. Over the next seventeen years,

A young Tony Hawk practicing tricks in a garage in 1987. *(Courtesy of John Storey/Time & Life Pictures/Getty Images)*

Hawk had seventy-three wins and nineteen second-place finishes in 103 events. He routinely dominated pro competitions in both street and vert (ramp) skating.

Hawk is credited with developing more than eighty different aerial skateboarding tricks. He was also the first pro skateboarder to land the "nine-hundred" (two-and-a-half aerial rotations before landing back on the pipe). Hawk accomplished that amazing feat during the 1999 Summer X Games. Since retiring from pro competitions, Hawk has put his name on a series of video games that have sold more than 12 million copies.

Skateboarding enjoyed its latest upswing in popularity with the introduction of the X Games in 1995. Skateboarding was one of the nine original sports in the first X Games. The first games were a huge success and introduced a large, new audience to vert skating. Writer and skateboarding historian Steve Cave claims that skateboarding's rise in popularity corresponded with punk music's increased popularity:

> Skateboarding started to grow again in popularity in the 90's, this time with a more raw, edgy, and dangerous attitude. This coincides with the rise of more

angry punk music, and the general discontent with the current system that raged throughout the time frame. Call it discontent, or call it Post Modern frustration, but the image of the poor, angry skater punk came to the surface loud and proud. Interestingly, this only helped to fuel skateboarding's popularity.

Recently, increased media attention and exposure, video games, and the growing popularity of skateboarding apparel have made skateboarding more mainstream. As more is being spent on the sport, more skate parks are being built and skateboarding companies focus on improving their products.

Among current skateboarders there's a decidedly mixed reaction to the idea of skateboarding becoming an Olympic sport. It looks likely that skateboarding will make its Olympic debut at the 2012 Summer Games in London. If it does, Shaun White will be twenty-five years old, certainly young enough to compete for a gold medal in the sport.

"I'm not for it at all," said skateboarding star Bob Burnquist. "I don't think that skateboarding needs the Olympics to be 'official' or anything like that. And I think it'll do more harm that good."

Skateboarding legend Tony Hawk has a different opinion: "I think that it would be good for the global recognition of skateboarding, and it might actually get people under forty to watch the Olympics again."

But Hawk acknowledged that the Olympic argument could negatively affect the sport. "My biggest concern is that it could currently divide the already splintered skateboard industry. We need more unity in our sport, not heated debates over the relatively small world of skate competitions."

Before skateboarding can become an Olympic sport, there are several unresolved issues that need to be settled. Several of them are the same ones that snowboarding had before its Olympic debut: how does one qualify for the competition; who decides on the rules; who will make the decision on how the course or the ramp will be designed? In competitions like the X Games and the Dew Tour, the athletes have usually been the ones to make those decisions.

Even after those issues are settled, there's yet another controversy about whether the Olympics will include street skating. Vert skateboarding may be more entertaining to TV viewers, but street skating has been more popular. Champion street skater Ryan Sheckler thinks that omitting his specialty from the Olympics would be a big mistake.

"I think that it would be [stupid] because street skating is just so fun to watch and has more following and more fans than any vert contest," Sheckler said.

For the past three years, the International Olympic Committee (IOC), the International Cycling Union (ICU), and the International Skateboarding Federation (ISF) have been meeting to find solutions to all the unsettled differences and unanswered questions. The ICU has been involved because the IOC has said that skateboarding is a wheel-based sport. Currently, the ICU is overseeing the debut of BMX biking competitions at the Beijing Summer Olympics in 2008.

ISF president Gary Ream explained:

> They want to protect us and make sure that if we are in the Games it's the industry making their own decisions, and that we show up for the Games as skateboarding is today. Obviously, there are Olympic rules and things that you have to do—they're not going

to throw those things out for us—but internally, within the sport we get to manage it. . . . So it's not so much of a choice. It's more like, "Let's organize and do it the right way because it's going to happen."

When skateboarding does become an Olympic sport, look for Shaun White to compete in it. Since he's a gold medalist in both the Summer and Winter X Games, he'll certainly want to become a gold medalist in both the Summer and Winter Olympics.

Four
Two Sports

Returning home victoriously from the Winter Games in Torino, Shaun didn't rest on his laurels; instead, he quickly threw himself into his second sport, skateboarding. It wasn't a smooth transition, though.

Although he started skateboarding first, Shaun White's dominant sport was always snowboarding; still, he never abandoned his love of skateboarding, and in 2001 he became a pro skateboarder.

In May of that year, he competed in his first pro skating event, the Slam City Jam in Vancouver, Canada. Shaun's fourth-place finish there allowed him to qualify for the Gravity Games and the Summer X

Games. Shaun finished ahead of several established powerhouse vert skaters, such as Bucky Lasek, Chris Gentry, and Mathias Ringstrom.

At that time, Shaun was more concerned about just enjoying himself than he was in winning. "It's all about having fun," Shaun said. "I just don't want to burn out before I turn seventeen."

As a professional competitor in two sports, Shaun has no off-season to rest and recuperate. Though snowboarding and skateboarding have their similarities, it's very difficult to make the transition from one sport to the other. Shaun explained:

> When I come back from snowboarding, I just can't do anything. I have kids come up to me saying, "You were so much better last year." I'm like, "Just give me a couple of days to get back on my skateboard." The whole first month, I need that time before the first contest to get strong and be able to do my tricks again. After that, I'm caught up and I have a whole other month just to go crazy. I feel so confident at that point. I feel that I can land everything.

Shaun won his first pro skateboarding event in 2002, at the Panasonic Open in Louisville. Yet his success

Shaun performs a trick during the 2003 X Games. *(Courtesy of AP Images/ Chris Polk)*

there didn't carry over immediately into the X Games. At the 2003 X Games, Shaun finished sixth in the vert competition. It would take him another two years to become a skateboarding medalist there.

Sometimes Shaun's willingness to try the most difficult tricks kept him from winning or placing higher. During the Best Trick competition at the 2005 X Games, Shaun used up all of his runs attempting the never-done-before 1080 (three complete airborne rotations). Shaun was never able to land properly. Still, he has many high profile supporters in the skating community, such as champion skater Tony Hawk.

TONY HAWK

Before he earned fame and acclaim as the world's greatest skateboarder, Tony Hawk was a headstrong and difficult child.

"Instead of the terrible twos, I was the terrible youth," Tony said. "I was a hyper, rail-thin geek on a sugar buzz. I think that my mom summed it up best when she said, 'challenging.'"

Tony Hawk *(Courtesy of Jaim Trueblood/Getty Images)*

As a child, Tony held himself to impossibly high standards. His skills and abilities didn't match up to how he envisioned himself, and failure hit him hard. After striking out in a baseball game, for instance, Tony hid in a ravine until his father coaxed him out. His parents decided to get to the root of the problem by having a school psychologist test him.

"The psychologist said that he had a twelve-year old mind in an eight-year old body," his mother recalled. "And his mind tells him that he can do things his body can't do."

Tony's brother, Steve, gave him his first skateboard. While riding it, Tony's body was able to do the things his brain said were possible. Skateboarding became the ideal outlet for Tony's energy and competitiveness.

"When he started getting good at skating, it changed his personality. Finally, he was doing something that he was satisfied with," Steve said. "He became a different guy; he was calm, he started thinking about other people and became more generous."

In spite of the personality changes, Tony was still his harshest critic. When he thought that he hadn't done his best in a competition, he would clam up and retreat to his room. If he spoke to anyone at all, it would be to his cat, Zorro.

"If I don't do my best it kills me," Tony explained.

Fortunately, Tony's parents remained patient and understanding. His father, Frank, supported Tony's efforts by driving him throughout California to compete at events. He built skate ramps for Tony to practice on; these ramps helped to popularize skateboarding. Frank played a major role in the founding of both the California Amateur Skateboard League and the National Skateboard Association.

After turning pro when he was sixteen, Tony enjoyed an incredible seventeen-year career where he was proclaimed as the world's greatest skateboarder. According to his online biography, Tony entered 103 pro competitions and won seventy-three. He also placed second in nineteen events. During that time, Tony made a lot of money, but he may have spent even more. When skateboarding's popularity began to wane in the early 1990s, Tony faced financial ruin.

However, Tony survived the financial setbacks and after skateboarding regained its popularity, he began signing lucrative endorsement deals with Jeep, Adio shoes, and Sirius Sateltie Radio. He also wrote a bestselling autobiography and put his name on a blockbuster video game series.

Although he's retired from competing, Tony still skates nearly every day. He works at learning new tricks and gives several demonstrations a year. Since becoming financially secure, Tony has generously given back to the sport that's given him so much. He created the Tony Hawk Foundation which promotes and helps to finance public skateboarding parks in low-income neighborhoods. The foundation has distributed more than $1.7 million to help establish over three hundred new skateboarding parks in the USA.

Most recently, Tony joined with Jeff Gordon, Cal Ripken Jr., Lance Armstrong, and eight

other prominent athletes to establish Athletes for Hope. The organization connects athletes, businesses, and individuals with charitable and community causes.

"Even five years ago, I thought Shaun was one of the most amazing athletes on the planet," Hawk said in 2001.

Not surprisingly, Shaun soon grew able to channel his skills into skateboarding, and in 2005, he won his first event in the Dew Tour. He also had a third-place finish in another Dew Tour event and won a silver medal in vert at the X Games.

However, after winning the Olympic gold medal in snowboarding, Shaun found it difficult to regain his momentum in skateboarding again. He was celebrating his well deserved victory and coping with more demands on his time for media interviews, endorsements, and celebrity appearances.

A newspaper article published shortly after the Olympics chronicled some of Shaun's many activities after becoming a gold medal winner:

White flew back from Italy after his Olympic victory
for a *Rolling Stone* cover shoot and to appear on talk
shows before returning for the closing ceremonies. In
the ensuing months, he hosted victory parties, made

Shaun makes an appearance on *The Tonight Show* after returning from
the 2006 Winter Olympics with a gold medal. *(Courtesy of AP Images/Mark
J. Terrill)*

celebrity gossip headlines when he was spotted with Lindsay Lohan, attended a movie premiere with Al Gore, snowboarded with Montel Williams and appeared in commercials for companies such as Hewlett-Packard and Target.

Shaun was surprised by how significantly his life was changed by winning the Olympic gold.

> I knew that it was going to be huge and I knew that I would get a lot of opportunities from that and a lot of success. But, I don't know, not to the degree that it's still going on. . . . My schedule has been slammed, but I couldn't be happier. That's what everybody dreams of, getting that one big break. And I feel like the Olympics did that for me.

But with all of those distractions, Shaun lost some of his focus on competing and learning new tricks, and was unable to give a full commitment toward perfecting his skills. When the skateboarding season began, Shaun was no longer at the top of his game.

"I went into skateboarding and I just didn't have anything left," he recalled.

During the first event of the 2006 Dew Tour, his first competition appearance since the Olympics,

Shaun shows his disappointment after finishing
in eighth place at the 2006 X Games. *(Courtesy of AP
Images/Jae C. Hong)*

Shaun finished last. His anger and embarrassment over his poor performance motivated him to win his next event.

But before long, he floundered again. At the X Games, he finished in eighth place out of ten skaters in the vert. In the best vert trick, he tied for fourth.

"At the X Games I was just disappointed at my skating," Shaun told an interviewer. "It was terrible."

Shaun dropped out of the Dew Tour and cut back on his snowboarding. In the winter of 2006-2007, he only competed in three snowboarding events; he won two. The limited snowboarding schedule enabled Shaun to focus on skateboarding and regain the edge he had lost by competing in two sports.

"The hardest thing for me is that I have to bounce back and forth between sports," Shaun said. "The hardest is just to kind of switch gears. During that whole time [snowboarding] the guys who are going to be competing against me were practicing, just skating."

Concentrating on skateboarding paid off. In 2007, Shaun returned to the Dew Tour and won the gold in the skateboard vert. A third-place finish at the Toyota Challenge in Salt Lake City clinched the title for Shaun.

Shaun competing in the 2007 X Games *(Courtesy of AP Images/Reed Saxon)*

Prior to that, he had won three vert competitions on the tour. He missed winning a fourth at the Toyota Challenge when he took a fall midway through his third run. It's expected that Shaun will defend the title next year, if he can continue to balance being a two-sport athlete.

five

The Future

At the age of twenty-one, Shaun finds himself in a peculiar place. As a professional athlete, it's expected that his best years are still ahead of him. Barring serious injury, Shaun could compete for another ten to fifteen years—maybe even longer. Yet, he's already won practically all of the honors, awards, and accolades that his two extreme sports have to offer.

Some of Shaun's admirers have wondered if he'd attempt switching from vert skating to street skating. Shaun, however, says he's not sure it would be a successful transition. He explained:

I love skating street. But I don't know if I could do it full-on. I skate for about three months [of the year] and during that time, I'm so bent on relearning all of my old tricks and trying to learn something new on the vert ramp that everything else just gets washed out. But at a certain point, I got really into hitting park handrails and doing kickflips over gaps and stuff like that.

Shaun has recently dabbled in surfing. With his natural abilities and talents, few would be surprised if Shaun became a star in that sport. But the demands of having to compete and try to excel in a third sport would probably be too much, even for him.

In his many interviews, Shaun hasn't said much about his future plans. Instead, he seems to prefer focusing on the present; and since he's financially secure, he doesn't really have to fret about his future. His endorsement deals for snowboarding and skateboarding equipment and apparel should continue to provide him with a steady income for years to come.

Indeed, Shaun's many major endorsement deals have made him a constant media presence, especially since his Olympic win. In addition to being seen with movie stars like Lindsay Lohan and Pamela

Anderson, and appearing on numerous magazine covers, Shaun has appeared in a number of TV ads. He's had specific ads built around him and his image for companies such as American Express and Hewlett Packard Computers.

Shaun has also appeared in several films and TV shows. He was the subject of the snowboarding and skateboarding documentary *The White Album*, released in November of 2004. He also appeared in *First Descent*, a 2005 documentary about the origins of snowboarding, especially its development into a professional sport in the 1980s. In that film, Shaun joined other noted snowboarders such as Hannah Teter, Shawn Farmer, Nick Perata, Terje Haakonson, and Travis Rice as they travel to the mountains of Alaska to snowboard on some previously untouched mountain paths, while reflecting on snowboarding's history and evolution. The film was the first produced by the Mountain Dew soda company. Shaun also lent his voice to Nickelodeon cartoon *Rocket Power*, and appeared on the TV prank show *Punk'd* on his nineteenth birthday.

The one goal that Shaun hasn't achieved yet is winning at least one more Olympic gold medal. If that happens again, Shaun says that he'll take a little more time to enjoy it.

Shaun has appeared in several TV shows and films, including *First Descent*, a snowboarding documentary. *(Courtesy of Universal Pictures/ ZUMA Press)*

"The first time it all went by so fast because it was just so exciting and I didn't know what to expect," Shaun said. "I think going back and re-establishing, trying to get another win, would be kind of setting it all in stone, which would be insane."

Shaun will undoubtedly continue to snowboard successfully, but even if he isn't able to win another Olympic gold medal, his place in the sport's history is assured. Barely out of his teens, Shaun has become one of snowboarding's first superstar athletes, and his influence and fame will undoubtedly attract many young people to the sport.

Regardless of what the future holds though, Shaun White continues to snowboard and skate for one very simple reason: he loves it. "I can have fun if there's a little snow bump, and me and my friends, we're just trying back flips and landing on our heads, you know what I mean?" he said. "Honestly, I think that the way to become the best is just to have fun."

Timeline

1986
Born September 3 in San Diego, California; undergoes surgery to fix medical condition, tetralogy of Fallot.

1992
Begins learning to ride a skateboard; learns to snowboard.

1993
Begins competing in amateur snowboarding events; finishes in eleventh place in twelve-and-under division of U.S. Amateur Snowboard Association National Championships.

1994
Meets Tony Hawk.

1993–1998
Regularly wins amateur snowboarding competitions.

1999
Begins pro-snowboarding career.

2001	Becomes a pro skateboarder.
2002	Wins two silver medals in Men's Snowboarding at the X Games.
2003	Wins two gold medals in Men's Snowboarding at the X Games; wins ESPY Award from ESPN for Best Action Sports Athlete.
2004	Wins two gold medals in Men's Snowboarding at the X Games.
2005	Wins gold medal in slopestyle Men's Snowboarding competition at the X Games; graduates from high school.
2006	Wins gold medal in Men's Snowboarding at the Winter Olympics; wins two gold medals for snowboarding at the X Games.

2007

Wins the Skate Vert championship in the Dew Action Sports Tour with three wins and two third-place finishes in five events; wins X Games gold medal for skateboarding.

(Photo courtesy of AP Images)

98

Sources

CHAPTER ONE: First Descent

p. 11-12, "Shaun White . . ." Sal Ruibal, "X Games upstarts now embrace the Olympics," *USA Today*, January 26, 2006.

p. 14, "[My mother] tells these stories . . ." Bill Ward, "The Quotable Shaun White," *Tampa Tribune*, February 13, 2006.

p. 14, "I rode on my knees . . ." "Board Meeting: Skateboarders Tony Hawk and Shaun White talk about style, attitude and the joy of riding," *Sports Illustrated for Kids*, June 1, 2001.

p. 15, "[Jesse] would say . . ." Ibid.

p. 15, "crazy on skis," Gavin Edwards, "Attack of the Flying Tomato," *Rolling Stone*, March 9, 2006.

p. 15, "Maybe on a snowboard . . ." Ibid.

p. 17, "Mozart was supposed to . . ." Ibid.

p. 17, "I gotta win all the games . . ." Ibid.

p. 17, "We almost didn't take him . . ." Mary Catherine O'Connor, "Interview," *MountainZone*.

com, http://classic.mountainzone.com/snowboarding
/2000/interviews/white/ (November 2007).

p. 18, "like five years in a row . . ." Edwards,
"Attack of the Flying Tomato."

p. 18, "Whenever I'm at school . . ." O'Connor,
"Interview."

p. 20, "My family took out . . ." Tyler Gray,
"White Out," *Men's Fitness*, December 2005.

p. 20, "We would shower at rest stops . . ."
Edwards, "Attack of the Flying Tomato."

p. 21, "I had made my parent's salaries . . ." Pete
Thomas, "One Hot 'Tomato,'" *Los Angeles
Times*, December 14, 2005.

p. 21, "The sport, which sometimes seemed . . ." Tim
Brooks and Earl Marsh, *The Complete Directory to
Prime Time Network TV Shows 1946-Present*
(New York: Ballantine Books, 1981) 644.

The History of Snowboarding

p. 28-29, "And then the kids kept . . ." "You Should
Thank The Man Who Built This Board," *Flakezine*,
November 10, 1994, http://www.flakezine.com/
poppen.html.

p. 29, "I built a lovely home . . ." Ibid.

p. 30, "Burton was calling his . . ." Ibid.

p. 30, "I just love to watch . . ." Ibid.

p. 36-37, "Once the province of . . ." Mary

Lord, "Snowboarding; Boarders will McTwist the night away at Salt Lake City, thrilled that their far-out sport is ready for prime time," *U.S. News & World Report*, January 28, 2002.

p. 38, "The guards were saying . . ." "Tomato Can!" *People*, February 27, 2006.

p. 38, "When I was younger . . ." Matt Higgins, "White Leads the Way In Making Helmets Cool," *New York Times*, March 19, 2006.

p. 40, "I've had parents say . . ." Ibid.

CHAPTER TWO: The Flying Tomato

p. 44, "defying both gravity . . ." Jodi Gallegos, "The X Games," *Extreme Sports Suite 101*, http://ExtremeSports. Suite101.com/article. cfm/The_X-Games.

p. 47, "I was more into Power Rangers . . ." Ruibal, "X Games upstarts now embrace the Olympics."

p. 49, "I think [riders] did it . . ." Ibid.

p. 51, "unassuming, goal-oriented," Thomas, "One Hot 'Tomato.'"

p. 51-52, "I definitely feel older . . ." Sean Littlejohn, "White On!" *Park & Pipe*, November 2005.

CHAPTER THREE: Olympic Glory

p. 55, "I was so mad . . ." Edwards, "Attack of the Flying Tomato."

p. 58, "I wasn't crying . . ." Ibid.

p. 58, "It hits you the next day . . ." Ibid.

p. 58-59, "When I saw my mom . . ." Michelle Hainer, "Don't Call Him the Flying Tomato!" *Teen People*, May 2006.

The History of Skateboarding

p. 63, "the most exhilarating and dangerous . . ." Tony Warshaw, *The Encyclopedia of Surfing* (Orlando: Harcourt, Inc., 2003), 543.

p. 66, "a new medical menace," Ibid.

p. 71-72, "Skateboarding started to grow again . . ." Steve Cave, "A Brief History of Skateboarding," *About.com*, http://www.about.com:skateboarding.

p. 72, "I'm not for it at all . . ." Pete Thomas, "Skateboarding goes for the gold," *Los Angeles Times*, June 24, 2007.

p. 73, "I think that it would be good . . ." Ibid.

p. 73, "My biggest concern is . . ." Ibid.

p. 74, "I think it would be . . ." Ibid.

p. 74-75, "They want to protect us . . ." Ibid.

Chapter Four: Two Sports

p. 77, "It's all about having fun . . ." Yi-Wyn Yen, "Double Ripper: At 16 Shaun White rules snowboarding," *Sports Illustrated*, July 7, 2003.

p. 77, "When I come back from snowboarding . . ." Justin Tejada, "White Hot Shaun White is enjoying life as an action sports superstar," *Sports Illustrated for Kids*, August 2006.

p. 84, "Even five years ago, . . . Edwards, "Attack of the Flying Tomato."

p. 79, "Instead of the terrible twos . . ." "Tony Hawk Bio," *Tony Hawk.com*, 2005, http:// www.tonyhawk.com/bio.html.

p. 81, "The psychologist said he had . . ." Ibid.

p. 81, "When he started getting good at skating . . ." Ibid.

p. 82, "If I don't do my best . . ." Ibid.

p. 85-86, "White flew back from Italy . . ." Vicki Michaelis, "White gliding in gold afterglow; Snowboarder-skateboarder likes extended air time," *USA Today*, January 24, 2007.

p. 86, "I knew that it was going to be huge . . ." Ibid.

p. 86, "I went into skateboarding . . ." Matt Higgins, "Out From the Cold, Snowboarder Tries to Duplicate Success," *New York Times*, July 26, 2007.

p. 88, "At X Games I was . . ." Ibid.

p. 88, "The hardest thing for me is . . ." Pete Thomas, "Drama at a minimum as Dew Tour winds down," *Los Angeles Times*, October 19, 2007.

CHAPTER FIVE: The Future

p. 92, "I love skating street . . ." Tejada, "White Hot Shaun White is enjoying life as an action sports superstar."

p. 95, "The first time it all . . ." Michaelis, "White gliding in gold afterglow; Snowboarder-skateboarder likes extended air time."

p. 95, "I can have fun . . ." Edwards, "Attack of the Flying Tomato."

Bibliography

"Athletes on the Edge 06." *Rolling Stone*, August 10, 2006.

Ciniglio, Tony. "White Puts It Together For One Last Run." *Los Angeles Daily News*, August 6, 2007.

Davis, James. *Skateboarding is Not a Crime: 50 Years of Street Culture*. Buffalo, N.Y.: Firefly Books, 1999.

Edwards, Gavin. "Attack of the Flying Tomato." *Rolling Stone*, March 9, 2006.

England, Dave. "Shaun White." *Snowboardermag. com*. http://www.snowboardermag.com/shaunwhite/.

Gray, Tyler. "White Out." *Men's Fitness*, December 2005.

Gregory, Sean. "You're Golden Dude!" *Time*, February 27, 2006.

Hainer, Michelle. "Don't Call him the Flying Tomato!" *Teen People*, May 2006.

Higgins, Matt. "No Snow, but White Still Provides the Sizzle." *New York Times*, August 6, 2007.

Hoffarth, Tom. "Getting Extreme With The Tomato." *Los Angeles Daily News*, August 6, 2006.

"Hot Tomato: Shaun White's otherworldly talents and trademark red hair make him the Boarder to watch in the Olympic halfpipe." *Sports Illustrated*, November 11, 2006.

Littlejohn, Sean. "White On!" *Park & Pipe*, November 2005.

Lord, Mary. "Snowboarding; Boarders will McTwist the night away at Salt Lake City, Thrilled that their far-out sport is ready for prime time." *U.S. News & World Report*, January 28, 2002.

Michaelis, Vicki. "White gliding in gold afterglow." *USA Today*, January 24, 2007.

"Out From the Cold, Snowboarder Tries to Duplicate Success." *New York Times*, July 26, 2007.

Relic, Pete. "Stronger, Faster, Mellower." *Rolling Stone*, August 9, 2007.

Ruibal, Sal. "X Games upstarts now embrace the Olympics." *USA Today*, January 26, 2006.

"Shaun White Profile." *About.com*. http://skateboard.
   about.com/od/proskatebios/p/ProShaunWhite.htm.
   "Shaun White wins first Dew title." *Grand
   Rapids (Mi.) Press*, September 24, 2007.

Tejada, Justin. "Board Meeting: Skateboarders
   Tony Hawk and Shaun White talk about style,
   attitude and the joy of riding." *Sports Illustrated
   for Kids*, June 1, 2001.

Thomas, Pete. "Drama at a minimum as Dew Tour
   winds down." *Los Angeles Times*, October 19, 2007.

"One Hot 'Tomato'; Shaun White, the U.S.' best
   hope to win Olympic gold in halfpipe snowboard
   event turns stylish acrobatics into a lucrative
   career." *Los Angeles Times*, December 14, 2005.

"Skateboarding goes for the gold." *Los Angeles
   Times*, June 24, 2007.

"The Tiger Woods of Extreme Sports." *Edmonton
   Journal*, September 28, 2006.

"Tomato Can!" *People*, February 27, 2006.

Ward, Bill. "The Quotable Shaun White." *Tampa
   Tribune*, February 13, 2006.

Warshaw, Matt. *The Encyclopedia of Surfing*.
   Orlando: Harcourt, Inc., 2003.

"White hot Shaun White is enjoying life as an

action sports superstar." *Sports Illustrated For Kids*, August 2006.

"White Leads the Way in Making Helmets Cool." *New York Times*, March 19, 2006.

White, Shaun. "Shaun White the 15-year old snowboarding phenom is stoked to drop into the Olympic halfpipe." *Sports Illustrated for Kids*, February 1, 2002.

Yen, Yi-Wyn. "Double Ripper: At 16 Shaun White rules snowboarding." *Sports Illustrated*, July 7, 2003.

Web sites

http://www.astdewtour.com

On this website, you can follow Shaun's progress in 2008 when he defends his skate-vert championship in the AST Dew Tour. The site also has videos, news of the tour, biographies of the athletes, and information on the skateboarding, BMX and FMX competitions on the tour.

http://www.transworldsnowboarding.com

The online version of the magazine features videos, photos, snowboarding news, product reviews, and reports on snowboarding resorts.

http://www.skateboarding.com

A website with skateboarding news, videos, photos, trick tips, interviews, and listings of skateparks in the USA and Canada.

http://www.white-wanpah.net

A fan site for Shaun's fans with a photo gallery, message board, and other features.

Index